HEPPLEWHITE SERPENTINE-BOMBÉ MARQUETRY COMMODE. With a clearly distinctive Dublin rear treatment. Victoria & Albert Museum. Crown Copyright.

THE MORE SIGNIFICANT GEORGIAN FURNITURE

THE MORE SIGNIFICANT GEORGIAN FURNITURE

F. LEWIS HINCKLEY

207 ILLUSTRATIONS

A WASHINGTON MEWS BOOK
Washington Square, New York

Other books by F. Lewis Hinckley

Directory of the Historic Cabinet Woods

Directory of Queen Anne, Early Georgian & Chippendale Furniture:
Establishing the Preeminence of the Dublin Craftsmen

Hepplewhite, Sheraton & Regency Furniture

Queen Anne & Georgian Looking Glasses

Metropolitan Furniture of the Georgian Years

Library of Congress Cataloging-in-Publication Data

Hinckley, F. Lewis.
The more significant Georgian furniture / F. Lewis
Hinckley.
p.   cm.
ISBN 0–8147–3461–8
1. Furniture, Georgian—Ireland—Dublin—Catalogs.   2. Furniture—
Ireland—Dublin—Styles—Catalogs.   I. Title.
NK2538.D8H554   1989
749.22′91835′074—dc20   89–22519
                                                          CIP

Contents

THE MORE SIGNIFICANT GEORGIAN FURNITURE 7

ANTIQUE FURNITURE OF FINE AND SUPERFINE
CAPITAL-CITY QUALITY 11

NOTES AND REFERENCES RE SOME
ILLUSTRATED EXAMPLES 15

FABRICATED TRIPOD FURNITURE 17

PLATES 19

INDEX 123

The More Significant Georgian Furniture

THE MORE SIGNIFICANT GEORGIAN FURNITURE is definitely not that which has been carefully documented as having been made for British royalty and nobility, by a surprisingly small number of craftsmen duly recorded as working in London during the eighteenth and early nineteenth century. After English researchists had traced their activities as far as possible, less creditable interests more frequently introduced typical Dublin productions as supposedly having been made in London, by either known or unknown craftsmen.

A much larger Dublin (than London) production of fine furniture and looking glasses was required, not only for countrywide distribution, but for shipments to England, Scotland, and Wales, as well as to ports in northern Europe and the West Indies. Tax-free looking glasses, in particular, were continuously supplied to the American Middle Atlantic and New England states.

Those extensive commercial activities may be equated to the ever-increasing numbers of such Dublin productions which, throughout the present century, have appeared in British and American museums and in English publications, mainly as "English" examples, but to a lesser extent as "extraordinary" or "superfine London" masterpieces.

The more significant Georgian furniture is therefore comprised of: (a) a wealth of misinterpreted Dublin productions which, as *Old English Furniture*, have so effectively and profitably been promoted by the London publishing industry; (b) the numerous mislabeled Dublin masterpieces presently exhibited as *English* in leading British, American, and other museums; plus (c) countless numbers of private acquisitions, especially those of American collectors, who have acquired many of the most interesting, decorative, and increasingly valuable Dublin importations, as continuously received here ever since the later decades of the nineteenth century.

In reality, antique English furniture per se, i.e. that made outside of the capital city, is so generally plain and uninspired, so undistinguished in its designs, as to hold little interest for collectors; nor can any real benefit be derived from its illustration, either for educational or advertising purposes. Had English museum furniture historians directed their attentions just to the London antique dealers' advertisements, and special articles published in the *Connoisseur* magazine, as far back as the earliest 1900s, they could not have remained so prejudicially misinformed about the subject of their supposed expertise.

Instead they would have found that at the turn of the nineteenth century London antique galleries were quite unable to meet the current demands of either English or American collectors for Queen Anne and Georgian furniture of the fine designs. These were readily available in the antique shops of Dublin, or sometimes through direct negotiations with owners of old Irish castles and mansions. They would have seen for themselves that as late as 1903 the premises of London antique dealers could not display such masterpieces, but instead were pictured as "richly stocked" with Dutch, Flemish, French, and Italian importations.

It might also have been realized through that generally overlooked but nevertheless most important documentary material, that English antique dealers did not enter the Dublin antique market until long after it had first become known to their American colleagues. Of these, Daniel Farr, with the most important gallery in New York City, had stopped going to Ireland after 1903, for with greater ease he could then obtain the same high-quality Queen Anne and Georgian furniture in London.

The English traders had also been preceded in Dublin by the more cognizant members of the British aristocracy, one of whom has proved to be of unusual corroborative interest in respect to the present researches. After more than sixty years of successfully supplying a continuous flow of books supposedly concentrated on the subject of Old English Furniture, the London publishing industry could not prevent the appearance of the first published evidence to refute that patently wrong and artfully misleading classification. That welcome support toward substantiating these researches was contained in Ralph G. Martin's biography of Lady Randolph Churchill, *Jennie*. In this he states that during her Ireland years (1877–1881) Lady Churchill was able to obtain choice pieces from ancestral homes in her rounds of the Dublin antique shops.

Thus the first published indication of Dublin's true significance in respect to its plentiful supplies of fine and superfine Queen Anne and Georgian masterpieces just happened to appear in a biographical publication, rather than in any of the numerous works supposedly concerned only with Old English Furniture. The very first mention of Dublin as a source of just Late Chippendale creations appeared in a brief note by Edwards and Jourdain in *Georgian Cabinet-Makers*, about Mack, Williams and Gibton, as "Upholsterers and Cabinet Makers to His Majesty, His Excellency the Lord Lieutenant and the Hon. His Majesty's Board of Works."

Despite the obvious international recognition of such an important Dublin firm, even its royal patronage was not commented upon by these leading English museum and literary authorities, whose own opus shows no such kingly recognition as having been bestowed upon any London firms. After giving the firm's 39 Stafford Street address in Dublin incorrectly as 39 *Stratford* Street, they merely noted that "Each of a pair of fine serpentine-fronted mahogany commodes, c. 1760, with elaborate brass rococo handles, formerly in the Samuel Courtauld Collection, bears the trade label of these makers."

Never having conceded the least importance to Dublin in its ordinarily expectable capacity as a large capital-city furniture center, they offered no further enlightenment such as that to be obtained through the usual channels in Dublin itself. Had they indeed made the proper inquiries they would then have learned that the Courtauld commodes could not have been made as they claimed, circa 1760, since that particular Dublin partnership did not come into existence until *1815*! Thus in keeping with Dublin's long-continued Chippendale vogue, lasting from the middle of the eighteenth to the middle of the nineteenth century, the Courtauld commodes are Late Chippendale examples, made between 1815 and 1825, and their elaborate rococo handles would also be of a Late Chippendale ormolu pattern.

With the working dates of Mack, Williams, and Gibton provided by John Teahan, Keeper, Art and Industrial Division, National Museum of Ireland, Edwards and Jourdain would also have received their first intimation of the Late Chippendale mode in Dublin seat furniture and cabinetwork. Had such information become general in English museum and literary circles, through investigations based upon the invaluable notice in *Georgian Cabinet-Makers*, plus the inevitable inquiries addressed to Dublin, a great overdependence on the misuse of "circa 1760" in regard to Chippendale furniture obviously made well after the middle decades of the eighteenth century might have been prevented.

That such information has not been carefully checked and evaluated would seem evident, since the still later nineteenth-century partnership of Williams and Gibton has in one instance been recorded as working at 39 Stratford [*sic*] Street, Dublin, *from the end of the eighteenth century*; and in another I have recently been thanked by an English furniture historian for calling attention to Edwards and Jourdain's notice "about W & G Mack."

It is indeed regrettable that those authors could not bring themselves to illustrate one of such an important pair of labeled Dublin commodes, of which I have been unable to obtain an illustration of any kind. Of course this would have been at odds with their long nurturing of the myth about Dublin's nonparticipation in the designing and execution of such fine capital-city masterpieces. Whatever their reason for not doing so, it was a futile passing over of clear and unquestionably contradictory evidence against their stand, especially in view of the other typical Dublin creations that they did in fact illustrate in *Georgian Cabinet-Makers*.

Among the most obvious of only Late Chippendale productions in the 1955 edition are: 97, a "Dressing-table, Based on a design in the *Director* (3rd Edition, 1762). Probably by Thomas Chippendale. From Kimbolton Castle, Huntingdonshire"—retaining its original Sheraton pressed brass knob handles* that were removed before its sale in New York; 125, a "Writing Cabinet on stand. From a design

---

* The recognition and classification of fine Dublin seat furniture and cabinetwork as Late Chippendale productions is still incomprehensible to unprofessional English authorities, one of whom has called such a designation as applied to a set of four very Late Chippendale armchairs from Trewergy Manor in Cornwall,** as "quite fantastic"! Nevertheless, even the most junior of such museum officials should be able to comprehend that the original Sheraton knob handles on the dressing-table mentioned above must point to, and at the same time verify, the complete and unassailable accuracy of its very late-eighteenth or early-nineteenth century origin.

in the *Director* (3rd Edition) dated 1760. Attributed to Thomas Chippendale"—also featuring Late Georgian handles; and, 133, a "Commode japanned black and gold"— with Late Chippendale open-fret gallery, etc., "Probably by Thomas Chippendale. Formerly in the Chinese Bedroom at Badminton House" *in Gloucestershire.***

** An important point of seeming insignificance, commercially, to English furniture historians, is the proximity of Dublin to old residences such as Trewergy Manor (in Cornwall), Badminton House (in Gloucestershire), and to many others situated elsewhere in England, as well as in Wales and Scotland.

Antique Furniture of Fine and Superfine Capital-City Quality

As ONE OF THE GREATEST CAPITAL CITIES of the eighteenth century, Dublin nevertheless stands alone in not being routinely acknowledged for the superb creativity and supreme excellence of the furniture produced there by its highly talented native and émigré craftsmen. Instead, with their great indifference to reality, English furniture historians have habitually claimed Dublin's fine and superfine Queen Anne and Georgian furniture as having originated in their own country, or even in its far removed capital city.

In contrast, Continental authorities have generally exercised great prudence in determining the authenticity of furniture as produced in their own capitals or major cities. Thus a great deal of truly scientific attention has been directed during the present century to such furniture, especially that of the capital cities in countries such as France, Italy, Germany, Belgium, Russia—even that of tiny Switzerland; while that of Ireland has been blindly disparaged as provincial in its entirety.

The all-British cooperative insistence on perpetuating the myth of Dublin as the only world capital entirely dependent on second-rate furniture does not accord with the presence of the finest Irish silver services, Waterford chandeliers, and the many other equally rich and decorative luxuries that have for so long been locally available to the wealthy owners of Irish castles and mansions.

Thus a primary concern of these particular researches has been to establish the unacknowledged importance of Dublin in comparison with London, Paris, Stockholm, Potsdam, and so on, during the eighteenth century. When it was finally realized that such determinations might easily be safely and indisputably indicated by consulting the pertinent records of populations, these were examined in their own special room at the Fifth Avenue branch of the New York Public Library.

There I was surprised to find out just how absurd it had been for otherwise well-educated English authorities to have so consistently ignored the true status of Dublin *vis-à-vis* that of London, from a demographic standpoint, and thus obviously also from sociological, geographic, and commercial points of view. Larger than any of the capitals of the Continent other than Paris, I found that after London, Dublin was formerly the third-largest metropolis of Greater Europe, and therefore of course in the entirety of the Western World.

When Continental *ébénistes* sought to further embellish their already perfected reservedly inlaid or marquetry masterpieces, they might accomplish such aims by an increased application of gilded brass (ormolu or *bronze doré*) ornamentation in the form of handles, escutcheons, moldings, panel borders, stile capitals, *chutes* and *sabots*. One of the most elaborately treated examples of this character, obviously made by an émigré *ébéniste* in Dublin, is illustrated in my *Metropolitan Furniture of the Georgian Years* (Pl. 13) as acquired by the Victoria and Albert Museum. There in a sequential arrangement it is preceded and followed by three Late Chippendale examples.

Late Chippendale furniture is that which was produced during the continued popularity of Chippendale designs in Dublin, after the regular Chippendale years and lasting until the middle of the nineteenth century. Since there was no such continuation in London it is obvious that all such Late Chippendale examples must have been produced in Dublin. However, the values of such productions may remain constant with those made during the middle of the eighteenth century, for indeed their makers had more time in which to improve their designing and working skills. This has been proven in various American auction sales of famous collections in which Late Chippendale examples have brought even higher prices than similar examples dating from circa 1750–1760.

Retail prices have also shown that American collectors are more appreciative of fine quality and designs when buying Queen Anne and Georgian furniture, than whether such offerings are incorrectly described as *English*, or whether they are properly and therefore more sensibly described as truly prestigious Dublin master-pieces.

Of the small Dublin Early Georgian carved, inlaid, and parcel-gilded walnut architectural secretaire, now in the Metropolitan Museum of Art, which R. W. Symonds illustrated (Fig. 64) in his *English Furniture From Charles II To George II*, he wrote: "I could not quote a better example of a good investment in English furniture than the scrutoire of all scrutoires, which was in the Percival Griffiths collection. Griffiths paid £1,000 for it in 1922, when a sum of four figures for a piece of English furniture was practically unheard of. After his death Griffiths' executors sold the bureau for £4,000, and now it is the star piece in the collection of Judge Irwin Untermyer of New York."

In comparison a somewhat larger Early Georgian carved, inlaid, and parcel-gilded walnut architectural secretaire illustrated (Pl. 91) in my *Directory of Queen Anne, Early Georgian and Chippendale Furniture*, accurately described as a Dublin masterpiece, was sold some years ago before the present devaluation of the currency, for "over a hundred thousand dollars." The buyer also requested, and was given, the dealer's own copy of the then, and still, withheld publication.

Another Dublin tour de force achieved the all time record selling price of $232,000. Illustrated in the former *Antiques World* for February 1980, this was a commode with *bronze doré* mounts of a true French Régence pattern, in which the top surface was inlaid with typical Dublin floral marquetry. Solely on the basis of those naturally and artificially tinted wood veneers, the piece had been attributed to the London work of Pierre Langlois.

Surely such an exceptionally farfetched attribution could not have fooled any of the major attendants at that sale, all of whose reference libraries would have included Edwards and Jourdain's *Georgian Cabinet-Makers*. There it is clearly indicated, and shown by his trade advertisement, that Langlois never claimed to be skilled in the usual Parisian, London, and Dublin style of wood marquetry work. Instead he sought patronage for his cabinets and commodes "inlaid in the politest manner with brass and tortoiseshell."

As he found, there was no interest in a revival of such boullework, and he soon returned to France, *circa* 1770. To coincide with the date of his departure English authorities have moved forward the *circa* dates of Dublin's grand serpentine-bombé marquetry commodes.* These were actually made *circa* 1775, long after Langlois had gone; or almost simultaneously with the marquetry pieces made by Chippendale between 1772 and 1775 for Harewood House.

A very different creation, also in no way comparable to any work actually carried out in London, is the fantastically shaped and richly mounted Victoria and Albert commode that has been mentioned above. Solely on the basis of two fraudulent metal "labels" that replace a former one, that particularly distinctive Dublin extravaganza, and a number of others in the same group, have been guilelessly accepted as having been made by a provincially trained craftsman whose work is absolutely unknown. It was publicized by the Museum as having been purchased for £5,000 with the help of a substantial grant from the National Arts Collections Fund, and a contribution from its supplier. Today in the New York City market a mate to that originally two-part library table might also bring about as much as the so-called Langlois commode, sold for $232,000; or even more according to the reactions of American auction goers to such exceptional opulence.

A less exuberant piece in the same group was described by R. W. Symonds in the *Leeds Arts Calendar, No. 39*, as *AN ENGLISH COMMODE OF A RARE DESIGN AND QUALITY*. In less than three small pages of text Symonds repeated the term *English* no fewer than seventeen times. Also, once the "English licensing authorities" had "recognized its importance," therefore no export license was granted to a collector in America. It therefore remained in England, as its presumed "Country of Origin."

In protesting too much that the Leeds Museum acquisition was *English*, without any heed in respect to its obvious capital-city quality, it would seem that Symonds still did not realize that there were only two such capital-city production centers in the entirety of the English and Irish provinces capable of producing such fine work: London of course, and the one he never recognized.

In fact, when he had stated, in a magazine article rather than in one of his more consequential publications, that "If a piece is known to have come out of Ireland it is accepted as having been made there," he still showed no realization that any such piece as he was referring to could only have been produced in the Irish capital city of Dublin.

* *Vide* my *Metropolitan Furniture of the Georgian Years* (Pls. 21 and 127).

English literary authorities and museum furniture historians must gradually realize that it can only diminish or seriously harm their authority when they cannot recognize, by design alone, that such plainly true Dublin masterpieces have *NOT* originated within their professed field of expertise. London productions have always been recognized and so labeled in English and American museums, and when also accurately shown in the literature. One hopes that pieces of such fine and superfine capital-city quality as those so mistakenly credited to Pierre Langlois and John Channon will soon be generally recognized as *NOT* being in any way representative of London designs and execution and that they will then be exhibited and published according to their own prestigious capital city of origin.

Indeed, to describe presently *any* Queen Anne or Georgian masterpieces as *English* is equivalent to doing their private, professional, or institutional owners a great disservice; as well as reflecting on the intellect of those who might be so hopelessly uninformed as to deny the prestigious significance of a definite capital-city origin, be it *either* London or Dublin.

Notes and References Re Some Illustrated Examples

Ill. 1 Pl. 1. Copied from a Dublin Early Georgian walnut example rather than from a supposedly English Queen Anne design. Another such example supposedly showing *Chinese influence* is illustrated in the *Dictionary of English Furniture*, Fig. 58, "From Warwick Castle."

Ill. 3 Pl. 1. With favorite Dublin shell-and-leaf carvings. *Vide* R. W. Symonds, *English Furniture From Charles II To George II*, Fig. 86, a similarly carved wing chair in original Irish needlework covering.

Ill. 4 Pl. 1. *Vide* also R. W. Symonds, *Furniture Making in 17th and 18th Century England*, Fig. 136.

Ill. 6 Pl. 2. In addition to all of its other distinctively shaped and carved elements, the most unmistakable handling of this masterpiece is the manner in which the arm terminals and their supports are whorled together, a treatment never followed in London or in any other furniture center of the eighteenth century. The chair brought $2,500 at auction some years ago, when that figure was equivalent to at least $10,000 in today's currency.

Ill. 10 Pl. 3. *Vide* R. W. Symonds, *English Furniture From Charles II To George II*, Fig. 82, with exact Dublin knee treatment. Collection of Lady Trevelyan, Welcombe, Warwickshire.

Ill. 11 Pl. 4. The Dublin design, carving, and gessowork attributed to James Moore of London, who died in 1726. *Vide* Edwards and Jourdain, *Georgian Cabinet-Makers* (1955), Pl. 32.

Ill. 14–15 Pl. 5. Dublin variations from London practices that have gone unnoticed by English authorities include the occasional use of inverse gadrooning, i.e. with the gadroons slanting toward, rather than away from, a central meeting point, as in 14 and 15 (*vide* also Ill. 24, 60, 66). With another, less frequent departure from the norm, in cable flutings reeds may depend, rather than rise (*vide* Ills. 96 and 131).

As a result of another such eccentricity, a London museum keeper illustrated a magazine article on the furnishings of a famous English residence with a Dublin Adam pier mirror shown as hanging upside-down. The inner oval frame was flanked by rising leaf scrolls and stems of foliations; these he had misconstrued as having been intended to point downward, i.e. to depend according to standard London practice. In confirmation of his faux pas the mirror reflected a corner of the room in which it had been improperly hung, with one corner of a chair back thus appearing as also suspended in an upside-down position.

Ills. 25–26–27 Pl. 9. Angular terminals of rear legs, as in Ills. 25, 26, 27, are helpful in comparative studies of Dublin versus London seat furniture. However, they (and also less sharply pronounced but widely flaring terminals, as in Ills. 13 and 14) should have greater significance to collectors of American furniture, for such treatments were not customary in this country. They have served in confirming the Dublin origins of a number of chairs that were otherwise in accord with designs brought here by Dublin-trained joiners, and which importing dealers in Americana had misrepresented as supposedly originating in New York, Boston, and Philadelphia.

Chairs and tables featuring leaf-carved cabriole legs with claw-and-ball feet (as in Ills. 17, 19, 20, 21, 65, 66) are often sought by such American dealers in the Dublin market.

While genuine American productions of such Early Georgian and Chippendale designs are often characterized by continuously rounded rear legs, in other instances the rear terminals may be narrowly flared, in keeping with those of Ills. 6 and 17 through 20. The heavier form (Ills. 13 and 24) was the only means through which a number of purportedly American chairs, featuring the so-called "Van Rensselaer back" with tassel splat, were conclusively determined as of Dublin, rather than New York origins.

Ill. 25 Pl. 9. With especially characteristic back, arm and leg treatments. *Vide* also Percy Macquoid, *Age of Mahogany*, 175–176, and Lord St. Oswald's Dublin chair-back settee-bed, 179; also *Dictionary of English Furniture*, Figs. 113–114.

Ill. 28 Pl. 10. In America Dublin-trained joiners combined this splat pattern with leaf-carved cabriole legs finishing in claw-and-ball feet, as in Ills. 17, 19, and 21.

Ill. 31 Pl. 10. The entire back pattern as copied in America was also combined with leaf-carved cabriole legs terminating in claw-and-ball feet. Specimens attributed to Benjamin Randolph of Philadelphia from *circa* 1760–1780.

Ill. 68 Pl. 30. A double-sided library table with lion-head pilasters, delivered from Dublin to Badminton House in Gloucestershire is illustrated (Pl. 102) in *Georgian Cabinet-Makers* as "Probably by Thomas Chippendale."

Ill. 73 Pl. 33. The popular Dublin fret pattern on both frieze and pilasters appears also on another double chest with all other equally characteristic Dublin features, illustrated in *Antiques*, January 1952, as made by Thomas Elfe in Charleston; the fret there being referred to as "Elfe fret on frieze."

Ill. 77 Pl. 37. Featuring characteristic Dublin fret patterns, moldings, and serpentine panels with corner leaf clasps of the type often associated with the names of Vile and Cobb. *Vide* Macquoid's *Age of Mahogany*, Figs. 139, 140; *Dictionary of English Furniture*, Fig. 37; and Jourdain and Rose, *English Furniture: the Georgian Period*, Fig. 83.

Ill. 83 Pl. 39. *Dublin-Hepplewhite* would be the most appropriate term in reference to Ills. 78 through 91, and to all related examples so typical of designs evolved in only that one particular capital city; while Continental-Hepplewhite would at least be more accurate than French-Hepplewhite.

Ill. 92 Pl. 42. A set of six sold as Philadelphia(?), XVIII Century. The same arm also appears in conjunction with a splat carved and pierced exactly as in the following example, Ill. 93.

Ill. 95 Pl. 42. The rudimentary claw-and-ball feet clearly documenting the structural configurations followed in innumerable Dublin, though never London, examples of such Hepplewhite seat furniture.

Ill. 99 Pl. 43. The design claimed as inspired by Robert Adam. Cf. Oliver Brackett, *English Furniture, Illustrated*, Fig. 216. "From Cassiobury Park."

Ill. 106 Pl. 45. *Vide* Macquoid and Edwards, *Dictionary of English Furniture*, Fig. 142, the same design described as "probably by Hepplewhite inspired by Adam"!

Ill. 137 Pl. 61. With top edge and stiles molded as in Ill. 136, the drawers inlaid with typical Dublin checkered link-chain bandings.

Ill. 139 Pl. 62. A Moore design such as one published by Percy Macquoid as *Irish* if not as a capital-city example, but the typical Moore inlays ignored by English authorities until the appearance of a larger example with similar frieze and stile inlays, accompanied by a bill from the maker. Moore worked for other, more highly skilled cabinet makers, his inlays also being represented in the sideboard table and pedestals with urns, in the Adam dining room of the Metropolitan Museum of Art, and in the commode here, Ill. 142.

Ill. 142 Pl. 63. The original handles, representative of the "finest British ormolu work," nevertheless not recognized heretofore according to their proper capital-city status.

Ill. 155 Pl. 74. Inlaid with multiple checkered bandings and stellate paterae. *Vide* also Macquoid's *Age of Satinwood*, Fig. 181, apparently by the same maker. This he recorded only as having been made for Queen Charlotte. According to its overall design, molded and banded treatments, frieze and swan-neck pediment, and the stellate inlays of those crowning scrolls, it was apparently made in the same Dublin shop.

Ill. 180 Pl. 84. One of a set of three made in 1816 for Princess Charlotte. Despite that recording the name and address of an individual or firm from which they were ordered would seem to have disappeared from the records through interests reaching no further than associations with royalty.

Ill. 186 Pl. 88. During the early days of these researches the number of sideboards displaying typical Dublin forms and decorative treatments, as in Ills. 184–186, became so great that twice all of the photographs and halftones were returned to the *Unproven* files, only to be satisfactorily proven over and over again.

Ill. 193 Pl. 92. The retention of such high-quality ormolu handles (cf. 142) and their contrived arrangements in relation to the decadent marquetry effects was so incomprehensible to English authorities that this, and several related cabinets have been "Attributed to Chippendale and Haig"!

Fabricated Tripod Furniture

THE MORE OBVIOUS FABRICATIONS of supposedly genuine Georgian tripod tables are shown in Plate 101, where these assemblages, through their present designs, proportional relationships, and other irregular effects should have been obvious to the highly respected English and American professionals through whose hands they have passed. The paw-foot base of Illustration 204 supports a pillar that, rather than being of one solid piece, has been fitted together from two separate leaf-collared sections, plus a plainly turned summital unit, segments that also vary slightly in their finished surfaces. The plain circular top piece with equal economy is edged with an easily accomplished bead-and-billet molding.

This concoction was accepted as a thoroughly genuine Early Georgian wine stand by one of the most prominent of former collectors, Percival Griffiths, by R. W. Symonds, a former leading authority, and by an internationally renowned firm specializing in Old English Furniture. It was published by Symonds in his *Present State of Old English Furniture*, and again in his more important work on *English Furniture From Charles II To George II*.

The more customary assemblages, effected by adapting tripod portions of pole screens as stands for genuine piecrust or plainer trays, are represented in Illustrations 205 and 206. In the latter example the assemblage is more noticeable because of the incongruous unit just beneath the "birdcage" frame, though this was undoubtedly viewed as consistent with his usual efforts by the overconfident supplier.

Regardless of their relative importance, otherwise, many fine tripod tables were originally supplied with plain circular tops. In various instances these have been scooped out to form a dished surface edged with a simple raised molding or one of piecrust form, narrower than the edgings in Illustrations 205 and 206, where the American practice is followed.

In general the scooping has been stopped short of a depth at which piercings by screws attaching the top to cross battens would be revealed on close inspection. Obviously this aim was not achieved with the dished top of Illustration 207, as indicated by the four covering inserts that appear in the newly formed surface. A prized exhibit in the famous Haskell Collection of Americana, its hypothetical valuation did not approach that of a more elaborate but similarly altered Dublin example from a smaller but more selective collection.

That example had been sold by a prominent New York City dealer as a thoroughly genuine American piecrust table. Its pillar was enriched with typical Dublin vine carving of the type represented here in Illustration 46. A narrow piecrust edging had been supplied in remaking the top, thus supposedly confirming its purported American origin. The principal steps in its conversion were noted in my appraisal: "The top has been reduced to so shallow a depth that holes remaining from original screws attaching it to cross battens may be discerned beneath its refinished surface. On the reverse side screws inserted through the flat parts of the metal housing for its snap catch have been reused, but only after reducing them to about half of their original length in order to prevent their also piercing the shallow depth of the re-turned top."

It is inconsequential whether or not marriages or other fabrications of this type are composed of elements that are identifiable as to their separate origins. In the great scarcity of tripod tables and stands that may be accredited to London, however, it would be unheard of to divide or change such examples in any way that might confuse their identities. Should they be loosely comparable in designs and quality to those produced in Dublin they would have additional rarity value, for at a very conservative estimate fewer than ten percent of all such tripod tables, pole screens, and so forth, were actually produced in London. The distinctive turnings, ogival tripods, and carving of Illustrations 205, 206, and 207 are certainly indicative of Dublin work. The top of Illustration 204 and all of its shaft being newly fashioned, the most that can be said for it in spite of its formidable authentications is that the paw-foot base is Dublinesque in character.

Plates

PLATE I

1 CHINESE DECORATED LACQUER SIDE CHAIR.
Exactly following a Dublin, rather than London,
Early Georgian walnut example. Nationalhis-
toriske Museum Paa Frederiksborg, Denmark.

2 EARLY GEORGIAN WALNUT ARMCHAIR.

3 EARLY GEORGIAN CARVED WALNUT SIDE CHAIR.

4 EARLY GEORGIAN CARVED WALNUT EAGLE-HEAD
SIDE CHAIR.

PLATE 2

5 EARLY GEORGIAN CARVED MAHOGANY CHILD'S ARMCHAIR.

6 EARLY GEORGIAN CARVED WALNUT ARMCHAIR. With Dublin's characteristic whorled–together arm terminals and supports.

7 EARLY GEORGIAN CARVED WALNUT SIDE CHAIR.

8 EARLY GEORGIAN CARVED WALNUT ARMCHAIR. Courtesy of Needham's Antiques, Inc., New York City.

PLATE 3

9   EARLY GEORGIAN CARVED WALNUT ARMCHAIR.
Courtesy of Needham's Antiques, Inc., New
York City.

10   EARLY GEORGIAN CARVED WALNUT
WING CHAIR. Collection of Lady Trevelyan,
Welcombe, Warwickshire.

PLATE 4

11 EARLY GEORGIAN GILDED CHAIR-BACK SETTEE. Metropolitan Museum of Art.

12 EARLY GEORGIAN CARVED WALNUT UPHOLSTERED SETTEE IN ORIGINAL NEEDLEPOINT. Courtesy of French & Co., Inc., New York City.

PLATE 5

13 EARLY GEORGIAN CARVED WALNUT EAGLE–HEAD ARMCHAIR.

14 EARLY GEORGIAN CARVED WALNUT SIDE CHAIR.

15 EARLY GEORGIAN CARVED WALNUT SIDE CHAIR. With favorite Dublin oak-leaf carving, cf. Ills. 16, 45, and 62; and inverse gadrooning, cf. Ill. 14.

16 EARLY GEORGIAN CARVED WALNUT UPHOLSTERED ARMCHAIR.

PLATE 6

17 EARLY GEORGIAN CARVED MAHOGANY EAGLE-HEAD SIDE CHAIR. With two pairs of eagle heads.

18 EARLY GEORGIAN CARVED MAHOGANY SIDE CHAIR.

19 EARLY GEORGIAN CARVED MAHOGANY EAGLE-HEAD ARMCHAIR.

20 EARLY GEORGIAN CARVED MAHOGANY UPHOLSTERED FLARE-ARM EASY CHAIR.

PLATE 7

21 EARLY GEORGIAN CARVED MAHOGANY UP-HOLSTERED OPEN-ARM EASY CHAIR.

22 EARLY GEORGIAN CARVED MAHOGANY WING CHAIR.

PLATE 8

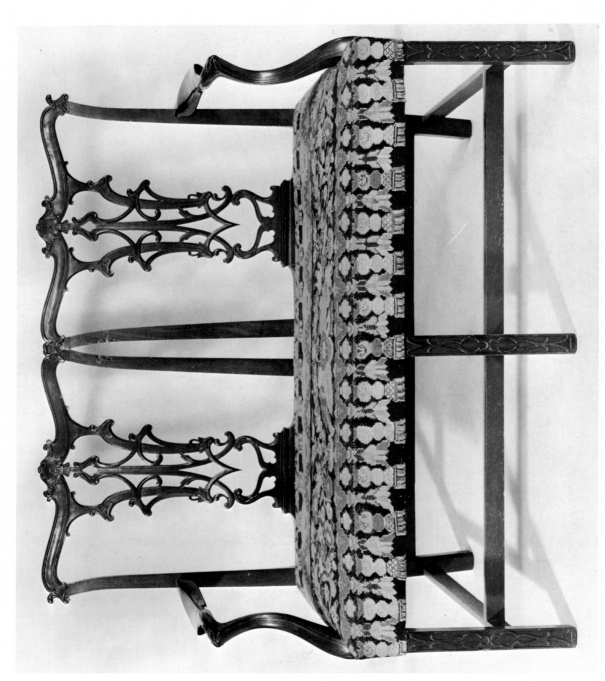

23 CHIPPENDALE CARVED MAHOGANY CHAIR-BACK SETTEE.

PLATE 9

24 CHIPPENDALE CARVED MAHOGANY SIDE CHAIR.
With inverse gadrooning, as Ills. 14, 15, 60, and
66. Victoria & Albert Museum. Crown
Copyright.

25 CHIPPENDALE CARVED MAHOGANY
RIBBAND-BACK ARMCHAIR. Victoria & Albert Museum.
Crown Copyright.

26 CHIPPENDALE CARVED MAHOGANY SIDE CHAIR.
Cf. Pl. 8.

27 CHIPPENDALE CARVED MAHOGANY
RIBBAND-BACK ARMCHAIR.

PLATE 10

28 CHIPPENDALE SHELL–CARVED MAHOGANY ARMCHAIR WITH GOTHIC SPLAT. The splat pattern also appearing in American furniture, c. 1770.

29 CHIPPENDALE CARVED MAHOGANY SIDE CHAIR.

30 CHIPPENDALE CARVED MAHOGANY EAGLE–HEAD ARMCHAIR.

31 CHIPPENDALE CARVED MAHOGANY ARMCHAIR. The entire back pattern followed in America, in combination with leaf-carved cabriole legs with claw-and-ball feet; some such examples being attributed to Benjamin Randolph of Philadelphia, *circa* 1760–1780.

PLATE II

32 CHIPPENDALE CARVED MAHOGANY ARMCHAIR.

33 LATE CHIPPENDALE CARVED MAHOGANY
SIDE CHAIR.

34 LATE CHIPPENDALE CARVED MAHOGANY
SIDE CHAIR.

35 LATE CHIPPENDALE CARVED MAHOGANY
SIDE CHAIR.

PLATE 12

36 CHIPPENDALE CARVED MAHOGANY SIDE CHAIR. Cf. R. W. Symonds, *English Furniture From Charles II To George II*, Fig. 166. Metropolitan Museum of Art.

37 CHIPPENDALE CARVED MAHOGANY ARMCHAIR. Collection of Joseph E. Widener, Philadelphia. Exhibited: Louvre, 1954.

38 LATE CHIPPENDALE FRET–CARVED MAHOGANY
UPHOLSTERED OPEN–ARM EASY CHAIR.

39 LATE CHIPPENDALE CARVED MAHOGANY
UPHOLSTERED OPEN–ARM EASY CHAIR.

PLATE 14

40 LATE CHIPPENDALE MAHOGANY ARMCHAIR
WITH PAGODA CREST.

41 LATE GOTHIC–CHIPPENDALE ARMCHAIR.

42 LATE CHINESE–CHIPPENDALE CARVED MAHOGANY SETTEE.

PLATE 15

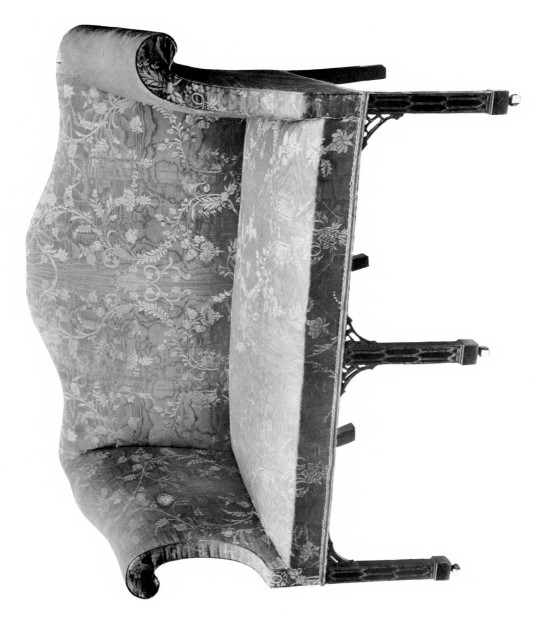

43 CHIPPENDALE FRET-CARVED MAHOGANY UPHOLSTERED SETTEE.

PLATE 16

44 CHIPPENDALE CARVED MAHOGANY TRIPOD
WINE STAND WITH PIECRUST TOP.

45 CHIPPENDALE MAHOGANY SMALL PIECRUST
TABLE WITH LION-PAW FEET. The tripod with
favorite oak leaf and acorn carving. Cf. 15, 16, 62.
Courtesy of French & Co., Inc., New York City.

PLATE 17

46 CHIPPENDALE MAHOGANY PIECRUST TABLE. The pillar and tripod with favorite grape vine carving.

47 CHIPPENDALE CARVED MAHOGANY TILT–TOP PIECRUST TABLE.

PLATE 18

48 CHIPPENDALE RICHLY CARVED MAHOGANY TILT-TOP TRIPOD TABLE WITH PAW FEET. Metropolitan Museum of Art.

PLATE 19

49 CHIPPENDALE CARVED AND GILDED CHEVAL SCREEN WITH TYPICAL IRISH NEEDLEPOINT PANEL.
Collection of Cora, Countess of Stratford. Victoria & Albert Museum. Crown Copyright.

PLATE 20

50 CHIPPENDALE MAHOGANY DECANTER STAND.

51 CHIPPENDALE MAHOGANY URN STAND.

52 CHIPPENDALE MAHOGANY LIBRARY STEPS.

PLATE 21

53 CHIPPENDALE MAHOGANY
SILVER TABLE.

54 LATE CHIPPENDALE FRET–
CARVED MAHOGANY SILVER
TABLE.

PLATE 22

55 LATE CHIPPENDALE FRET-CARVED MAHOGANY SILVER TABLE.

56 LATE CHIPPENDALE FRET-CARVED MAHOGANY SILVER TABLE.

PLATE 23

57 GEORGE III MAHOGANY DROP–LEAF
SPIDER–LEG TABLE.

58 GEORGE III MAHOGANY
DROP–LEAF SPIDER–LEG TABLE.
Misrepresented as American
example.

PLATE 24

59 LATE CHIPPENDALE FRET-CARVED MAHOGANY DOUBLE-SIDED WRITING TABLE. With original handles of a typical Late Chippendale pattern. Courtesy of Needham's Antiques, Inc., New York City.

PLATE 25

60 EARLY GEORGIAN CARVED WALNUT CARD TABLE. With inverse gadrooning.

61 EARLY GEORGIAN CARVED WALNUT CARD TABLE.

PLATE 26

62 EARLY GEORGIAN INLAID WALNUT SERPENTINE-FRONT CARD TABLE WITH PAW FEET. The knees carved with oak leaves; cf. Ills. 15, 16, and 45.

63 EARLY GEORGIAN CARVED MAHOGANY SERPENTINE-FRONT CARD TABLE.

PLATE 27

64 CHIPPENDALE CARVED
MAHOGANY CARD TABLE. With
distinctive ribbon-and-rosette
top edge carving, knees, and
whorl feet.

65 CHIPPENDALE CARVED
MAHOGANY DROP-LEAF SIDE
TABLE. Cf. legs and feet with
Ill. 19, 21, and 47 and with
chairs and tables throughout
the literature on Early American furniture.

PLATE 28

66 CHIPPENDALE CARVED MAHOGANY SIDE TABLE. With inverse gadrooning. Metropolitan Museum of Art.

PLATE 29

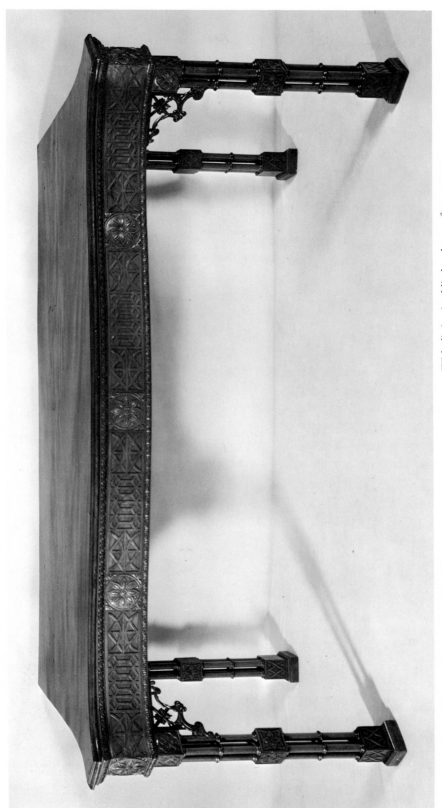

67 LATE CHIPPENDALE FRET-CARVED MAHOGANY SIDE TABLE. With distinctive blind and open-fret patterns, and cluster-column supports.

PLATE 30

68 LATE GEORGIAN CARVED MAHOGANY LIBRARY TABLE. The type ascribed to William Kent and William Vile throughout the literature, but made in Dublin up until the Victorian years, along with the Late Chippendale productions. Collection of Viscount Downe, Wykeham Abbey, Yorkshire.

PLATE 31

69 LATE CHIPPENDALE ELABO-
RATELY SHAPED AND CARVED
MAHOGANY "DIRECTOR" COM-
MODE. With original front and
side mounts. Collection of the
Marquess of Ripon, Studleigh
Royal, Yorkshire.

70 LATE CHIPPENDALE CARVED MAHOGANY
SERPENTINE-FRONT COMMODE. With original
handles. Collection of Sir George Lindsay,
Holford, Tetbury, Gloucestershire.

PLATE 32

71 CHINESE-CHIPPENDALE
OPEN-FRET HANGING SHELVES.

72 LATE CHIPPENDALE CARVED
MAHOGANY SERPENTINE-FRONT
COMMODE.

PLATE 33

73 LATE CHIPPENDALE FRET-CARVED MAHOGANY CHEST-ON-CHEST.

PLATE 34

74 CHIPPENDALE MAHOGANY SLANT-FRONT SECRETAIRE. Courtesy of Needham's Antiques, Inc., New York City.

PLATE 35

75 LATE CHIPPENDALE MAHOGANY SECRETAIRE.

PLATE 36

76 LATE CHIPPENDALE MAHOGANY BREAKFRONT BOOKCASE.

PLATE 37

77 LATE CHIPPENDALE CARVED MAHOGANY BREAKFRONT BOOKCASE.

PLATE 38

78 HEPPLEWHITE MAHOGANY WINDOW SEAT.

79–80 PAIR HEPPLEWHITE MAHOGANY STOOLS.

81 HEPPLEWHITE MAHOGANY ARMCHAIR.

82 HEPPLEWHITE MAHOGANY ARMCHAIR.

PLATE 39

83   DUBLIN–HEPPLEWHITE MAHOGANY ARMCHAIR.

84   DUBLIN–HEPPLEWHITE MAHOGANY ARMCHAIR.

85   DUBLIN–HEPPLEWHITE MAHOGANY ARMCHAIR.

86   DUBLIN–HEPPLEWHITE MAHOGANY ARMCHAIR.

PLATE 40

87 HEPPLEWHITE MAHOGANY WINDOW SEAT. Courtesy of Needham's Antiques, Inc., New York City.

88 HEPPLEWHITE MAHOGANY SMALL SETTEE.

PLATE 41

89 HEPPLEWHITE BEECHWOOD ARMCHAIR.

90 HEPPLEWHITE BEECHWOOD ARMCHAIR.

91 HEPPLEWHITE PAINTED BEECHWOOD SETTEE.

PLATE 42

92 HEPPLEWHITE MAHOGANY ARMCHAIR. Sold as a "Philadelphia" example.

93 HEPPLEWHITE MAHOGANY ARMCHAIR. With "Philadelphia" splat.

94 HEPPLEWHITE MAHOGANY HORSESHOE ARMCHAIR.

95 HEPPLEWHITE MAHOGANY TUB CHAIR. With serpentine seat molding curving into cabriole legs with ball-and-claw feet.

PLATE 43

96 HEPPLEWHITE MAHOGANY ARMCHAIR.

97 HEPPLEWHITE MAHOGANY SIDE CHAIR. With ribband-carved splat. Victoria & Albert Museum. Crown Copyright.

98 HEPPLEWHITE MAHOGANY SIDE CHAIR. Also with ribband-carved splat.

99 HEPPLEWHITE MAHOGANY SIDE CHAIR. The design claimed as inspired by Robert Adam. Cf. Oliver Brackett, *English Furniture Illustrated*, 216, "From Cassiobury Park."

PLATE 44

100 HEPPLEWHITE MAHOGANY SIDE CHAIR WITH PRINCE-OF-WALES PLUMES.

101 HEPPLEWHITE INLAID MAHOGANY SIDE CHAIR.

102 HEPPLEWHITE MAHOGANY SIDE CHAIR. Courtesy of J. J. Wolff (Antiques) Ltd., New York City.

103 HEPPLEWHITE MAHOGANY ARMCHAIR. *Vide* also Macquoid's *Age of Satinwood*, Fig. 179.

PLATE 45

104 HEPPLEWHITE MAHOGANY ARMCHAIR.

105 HEPPLEWHITE MAHOGANY SIDE CHAIR.

106 HEPPLEWHITE MAHOGANY ARMCHAIR.

107 HEPPLEWHITE MAHOGANY ARMCHAIR.

PLATE 46

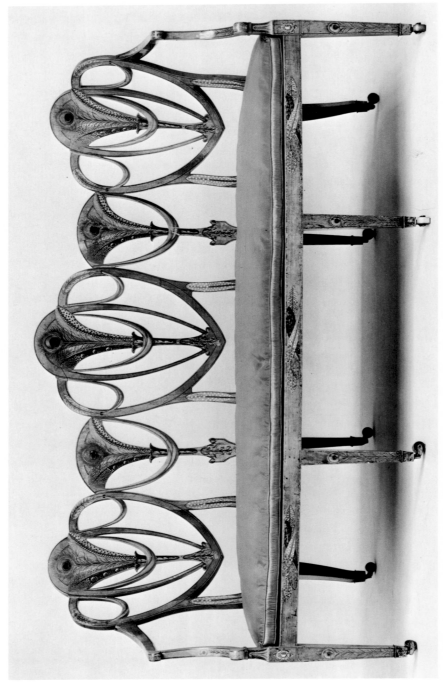

108   HEPPLEWHITE DECORATED SATINWOOD CHAIR–BACK SETTEE.   Metropolitan Museum of Art.

PLATE 47

109 HEPPLEWHITE PAINTED AND DECORATED ARMCHAIR. Sold as "Venetian."

110 HEPPLEWHITE PAINTED AND DECORATED SIDE CHAIR.

111 HEPPLEWHITE PAINTED AND DECORATED ARMCHAIR.

112 HEPPLEWHITE CARVED, PAINTED, AND DECORATED ARMCHAIR. Victoria & Albert Museum. Crown Copyright.

PLATE 48

113   HEPPLEWHITE MARQUETRY SLANT–FRONT
WRITING TABLE. Courtesy of French & Co., Inc.,
New York City.

114   HEPPLEWHITE INLAID MAHOGANY DRESSING
TABLE.

PLATE 49

115 HEPPLEWHITE MARQUETRY DRESS-
ING TABLE. Victoria & Albert Museum. Crown Copyright.

116 OPEN VIEW OF DRESSING TABLE.
Victoria & Albert Museum. Crown
Copyright.

PLATE 50

117   HEPPLEWHITE MARQUETRY WRITING TABLE.

118   HEPPLEWHITE MARQUETRY TAMBOUR WRITING TABLE. Metropolitan Museum of Art.

PLATE 51

119 HEPPLEWHITE MAHOGANY DRAW-LEAF WRITING TABLE. Courtesy of Needham's Antiques, Inc., New York City.

120 GEORGE III MAHOGANY PEDESTAL DESK. With original front and side carrying handles.

PLATE 52

121   DUBLIN–HEPPLEWHITE
MAHOGANY CONSOLE.

122   DUBLIN–HEPPLEWHITE INLAID
MAHOGANY CARD TABLE-CONSOLE.
Courtesy of Trevor, London.

PLATE 53

123 HEPPLEWHITE INLAID
HAREWOOD AND SATINWOOD CARD
TABLE. Displaying the characteristic
inlays of William Moore.

124 HEPPLEWHITE INLAID SYCAMORE
CONSOLE TABLE.

PLATE 54

125 HEPPLEWHITE PAINTED AND DECORATED PIER TABLE.

PLATE 55

126 HEPPLEWHITE GILDED CONSOLE WITH INLAID SATINWOOD TOP. Courtesy of Needham's Antiques, Inc., New York City.

127 HEPPLEWHITE PAINTED, DECORATED, AND GILDED CONSOLE TABLE. The top painted on copper.

PLATE 56

128 ONE SECTION OF A TWO-PART HEPPLEWHITE MAHOGANY DINING TABLE. With identifying frieze and leg treatments and checkered top banding. Victoria & Albert Museum. Crown Copyright.

129 HEPPLEWHITE MAHOGANY SIDEBOARD TABLE.

PLATE 57

130   HEPPLEWHITE INLAID MAHOGANY SIDE TABLE. The frieze enhanced with typical Moore inlays.

131   GEORGE III CARVED MAHOGANY SIDE TABLE. With festooned satyr mask, the legs fashioned with drop reeds. Metropolitan Museum of Art.

PLATE 58

132 GEORGE III MAHOGANY SIDEBOARD.

PLATE 59

133 HEPPLEWHITE DECORATED LACQUER COMMODE. With especially distinctive ormolu stile mounts and top edging. Victoria & Albert Museum. Crown Copyright.

134 GEORGE III (SO-CALLED CHARLES II) DECORATED BLACK AND TORTOISESHELL LACQUER CABINET. With modern base of an appropriate Late Georgian design.

PLATE 60

135 HEPPLEWHITE MAHOGANY COMMODE.

136 HEPPLEWHITE MAHOGANY WRITING AND DRESSING COMMODE. In the Dublin-Hepplewhite, rather than *French* taste.

PLATE 61

137 HEPPLEWHITE INLAID
MAHOGANY DRESSING COMMODE. The
top edge and stile molding as in Ill.
136, the drawers paneled with a typical Dublin checkered link-chain banding. Victoria & Albert Museum.
Crown Copyright.

138 HEPPLEWHITE MAHOGANY CHEST
OF DRAWERS.

PLATE 62

139 HEPPLEWHITE INLAID SYCAMORE AND SATINWOOD COMMODE. Made by William Moore. Courtesy of Mallett & Son (Antiques) Ltd., London and Geneva.

140 HEPPLEWHITE INLAID SATIN-WOOD COMMODE. Made by William Moore.

PLATE 63

141 HEPPLEWHITE SYCAMORE AND SATINWOOD MARQUETRY COMMODE. Made by William Moore. Victoria & Albert Museum. Crown Copyright.

142 HEPPLEWHITE MAHOGANY SERPENTINE-FRONT COMMODE. Inlaid by William Moore; the handles representative of the "Finest British ormolu work," as produced in Dublin. Courtesy of French & Co., Inc., New York City.

PLATE 64

143 SHERATON SATINWOOD AND
HOLLY MARQUETRY ENCOIGNURE.

144 SHERATON SATINWOOD AND
HOLLY MARQUETRY COMMODE. Made
by William Moore.

PLATE 65

145 SHERATON MARQUETRY HANGING
SHELVES.

146 HEPPLEWHITE FRET–CARVED AND
INLAID HANGING SHELVES.

PLATE 66

147 SHERATON INLAID MAHOGANY PIER CABINET. Courtesy of Needham's Antiques, Inc., New York City.

PLATE 87

148   GEORGE III INLAID MAHOGANY WARDROBE CABINET.

PLATE 68

149 GEORGE III MAHOGANY SECRETAIRE.

PLATE 89

150   GEORGE III CARVED AND INLAID MAHOGANY SECRETAIRE.

PLATE 70

151 GEORGE III FRET–CARVED AND INLAID MAHOGANY SECRETAIRE.

PLATE 71

152 GEORGE III FRET-CARVED AND INLAID MAHOGANY SECRETAIRE. With original rams-head urn handles; the small drawers faced with Irish yew. From the Earl of Warwick, Warwick Castle, Warwickshire.

PLATE 72

153 GEORGE III INLAID SATINWOOD SECRETAIRE.

PLATE 73

154   SHERATON INLAID SATINWOOD SECRETAIRE.

PLATE 74

155 SHERATON INLAID AMARILLO BREAKFRONT BOOKCASE. Inlaid with multiple checkered bandings and stellate paterae. *Vide* also *Age of Satinwood*, Fig. 181, apparently by the same maker.

PLATE 75

156 SHERATON MAHOGANY SIDE CHAIR.

157 SHERATON MAHOGANY SIDE CHAIR
WITH COMPASS SEAT.

158 SHERATON MAHOGANY SIDE CHAIR.

159 SHERATON MAHOGANY ARMCHAIR.

PLATE 76

160 SHERATON MAHOGANY UPHOLSTERED
TUB CHAIR.

161 SHERATON MAHOGANY
UPHOLSTERED TUB CHAIR.

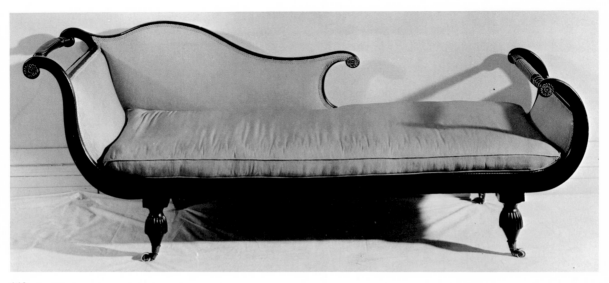

162 REGENCY EBONIZED CHAISE LONGUE.

PLATE 77

163 SHERATON PAINTED AND DECORATED
ARMCHAIR.

164 SHERATON PAINTED AND DECORATED
ARMCHAIR.

165 REGENCY BLACK-AND-GOLD ARMCHAIR.

166 REGENCY BLACK-AND-GOLD ARMCHAIR WITH
PAINTED DECORATIONS. Victoria & Albert
Museum. Crown Copyright.

PLATE 78

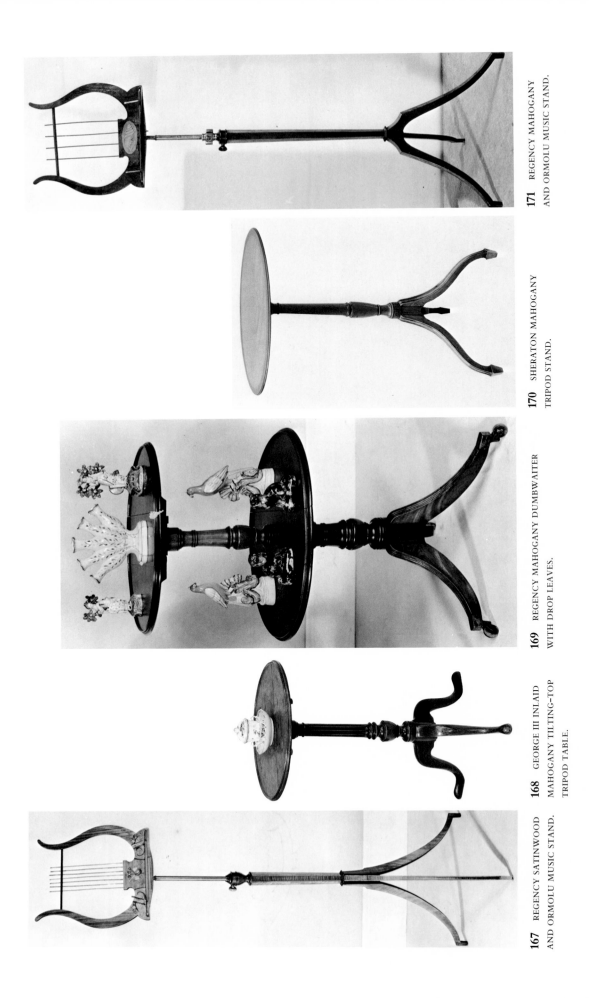

171 REGENCY MAHOGANY AND ORMOLU MUSIC STAND.

170 SHERATON MAHOGANY TRIPOD STAND.

169 REGENCY MAHOGANY DUMBWAITER WITH DROP LEAVES.

168 GEORGE III INLAID MAHOGANY TILTING-TOP TRIPOD TABLE.

167 REGENCY SATINWOOD AND ORMOLU MUSIC STAND.

PLATE 79

174 REGENCY MAHOGANY REVOLVING BOOKSTAND WITH ORMOLU GALLERY.

173 REGENCY MAHOGANY DUMBWAITER.

172 REGENCY MAHOGANY AND ORMOLU DUMBWAITER.

PLATE 80

175 REGENCY INLAID MAHOGANY DRUM TABLE.

PLATE 81

176 REGENCY MAHOGANY PEDESTAL BREAKFAST TABLE.

PLATE 82

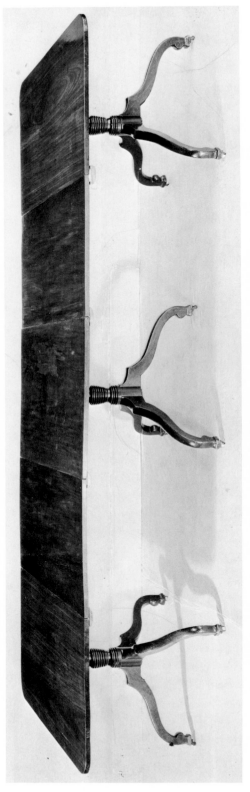

177 REGENCY MAHOGANY THREE-PEDESTAL DINING TABLE.

PLATE 83

178 REGENCY ROSEWOOD SOFA TABLE MOUNTED IN ORMOLU.

179 REGENCY INLAID ROSEWOOD SOFA-WRITING TABLE.

PLATE 84

180 REGENCY BRASS-INLAID AMBOINA SOFA TABLE. One of three made in 1816 for Princess Charlotte. Victoria & Albert Museum. Crown Copyright.

PLATE 85

181 REGENCY MAHOGANY DOUBLE-SIDED BOOKSTAND.

PLATE 86

182 SHERATON INLAID SATINWOOD
BONHEUR DU JOUR. Victoria & Albert
Museum. Crown Copyright.

183 REGENCY INLAID SATINWOOD
CYLINDER–FRONT WRITING CABINET.

PLATE 87

184 SHERATON INLAID MAHOGANY SERVING TABLE.

185 SHERATON INLAID MAHOGANY SMALL SIDEBOARD.

PLATE 88

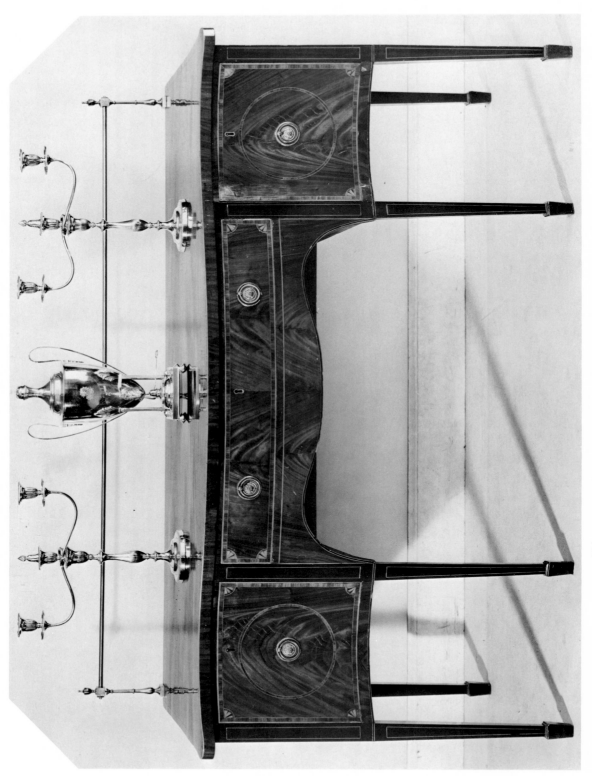

186 SHERATON INLAID MAHOGANY SIDEBOARD WITH ORMOLU GALLERY.

PLATE 89

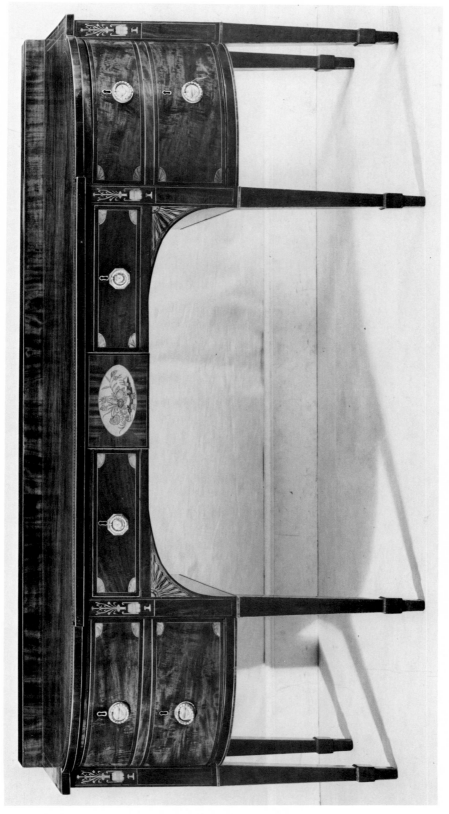

187 SHERATON INLAID MAHOGANY SIDEBOARD WITH REAR PLATEAU.

PLATE 90

188 SHERATON INLAID
MAHOGANY CHEST-OF-DRAWERS.
Courtesy of Needham's Antiques, Inc.,
New York City.

189 SHERATON MAHOGANY CHEST-
OF-DRAWERS.

PLATE 91

190   GEORGE III INLAID SATINWOOD
AND ROSEWOOD COMMODE WITH
ORMOLU GALLERY. Metropolitan
Museum of Art.

191   GEORGE III INLAID SYCAMORE
AND BIRD'S-EYE MAPLE COMMODE.

PLATE 92

192 GEORGE III CARVED AND EBONIZED YEWWOOD
WRITING CABINET.

193 GEORGE III MARQUETRY WRITING CABINET.

PLATE 93

194 REGENCY INLAID MAHOGANY OPEN-SHELF CABINET WITH
GRILLE PANELS.

PLATE 94

195 REGENCY INLAID
ROSEWOOD OPEN-SHELF
CABINET WITH GRILLE PANELS.

196 REGENCY INLAID
ROSEWOOD BREAKFRONT
CABINET.

PLATE 95

197 REGENCY BRASS–INLAID AND ORMOLU–MOUNTED ROSEWOOD OPEN– SHELF CABINET.

198 REGENCY BRASS–INLAID ROSEWOOD DWARF CABINET.

PLATE 96

199   SHERATON INLAID MAHOGANY PIER CABINET.

PLATE 97

200   SHERATON INLAID MAHOGANY PIER CABINET.

PLATE 98

201   SHERATON INLAID MAHOGANY BOW-FRONT SECRETAIRE.
Courtesy of Needham's Antiques, Inc., New York City.

PLATE 99

202 SHERATON INLAID MAHOGANY SECRETAIRE.

PLATE 100

203   SHERATON INLAID MAHOGANY BREAKFRONT BOOKCASE.

PLATE 121

204 A SUPPOSEDLY ANTIQUE EARLY
GEORGIAN WINE STAND.

205 A SUPPOSEDLY GENUINE CHIPPENDALE
PIECRUST TABLE.

206 A SUPPOSEDLY GENUINE CHIPPENDALE
TILT–TOP PIECRUST TABLE.

207 A SUPPOSEDLY GENUINE CHIPPENDALE CARVED
MAHOGANY TRIPOD TABLE. With recently dished top.

Index

[Italic figures refer to illustrations]

Adam, Robert, 16, *99*
Age of Mahogany, 16
Age of Satinwood, 16, *103*
America, 7, 16, *31*
American back pattern, 15–16
American chairs, 15–16
American collectors, 7, 12
American dealers, 15
American example, *58*
American furniture, 15, *28*
American museums, 7, 14
American productions, 15–16
Antiques, 16
Antiques World, 12

Badminton House, 10, 16
Banding, checkered, *128, 137, 155*
Belgium, 11
Bird's-eye maple, *191*
boullework, 13
Boston, 15
Brackett, Oliver, *99*
British aristocracy, 8
British nobility, 7
British royalty, 7
Bronze doré, 12

Capital-city quality, 11
Cassiobury Park, 16, *99*
Channon, John, 14
Charlemont, Earl of, *Frontispiece*
Charlemont House, *Frontispiece*
Charleston, 16
Charlotte, Princess, 16, *180*
Charlotte, Queen, 16
Checkered banding, *128, 137, 155*
Chinese, *1*

Chippendale, Thomas, 9, 13, 16
Chippendale and Haig, 16
Churchill, Lady Randolph, 8
Circa dates, 8, 13
Connoisseur, 8
Continental *ébénistes*, 12
Copper, painting on, *127*
Cornwall, 10
"Country of Origin," 13
Courtauld Collection, 8
Courtauld commodes, 9

Dictionary of English Furniture, 15, 16
Director, Chippendale's, 9, *69*
Directory of Queen Anne, Early Georgian and Chippendale Furniture, 12
Downe, Viscount, *68*
Drop reeds, *131*
Dublin, 7–9, 11–14, 16
Dublin antique market, 8
Dublin checkered link-chain bandings, 16
Dublin creations, 9
Dublin firm, 8
Dublin floral marquetry, 12
Dublin fret pattern, 16
Dublin-Hepplewhite taste, *136*
Dublin importations, 7
Dublin market, 15
Dublin marquetry, 13
Dublin origins, 15, 16
Dublin partnership, 9
Dublin productions, 7
Dublin's Chippendale vogue, long continued, 9
Dublin's true significance, 8
Dublin-trained craftsmen, 15, 16
Dutch furniture, 8

Edwards and Jourdain, 8, 9, 13, 15
Elfe, Thomas, 16
England, 7, 13
English (misnomer), 7, 12, 13, 14
English authorities, 8, 15, 16
English furniture per se, 7
English furniture historians, 7–9, 11, 14
English Furniture, Illustrated, 99
English Furniture: the Georgian Period, 16
*English Furniture From Charles II to George
    II*, 12, 15, 17, *36*
English licensing authorities, 13
English literary authorities, 14
English museums, 14
English provinces, 13
English traders, 8

Fabrications of tripod furniture, 17
Farr, Daniel, 8
Flemish furniture, 8
France, 11
French furniture, 8
French Régence pattern, 12
*Furniture Making in 17th and 18th Century
    England*, 15

Gadrooning, inverse, *15, 60, 66*
Georgian Cabinet-Makers, 8–9, 13, 15, 16
Germany, 11
Gloucestershire, 10, 16, *70*
Grape-vine carving, *46*
Griffiths, Percival, 12, 17

Handles, 8, 9, 12, 16
Handles, Dublin, *59, 120, 142, 152*
Harewood House, 13
Haskell Collection, 18

Importing dealers in Americana, 15
Inverse gadrooning, 15
Ireland, 8, 13
Irish castles and mansions, 8, 11
Irish needlework, 15
Irish provinces, 13
Irish silver services, 11
Italian furniture, 8
Italy, 11

Jennie, 8
Jourdain and Rose, 16

Kent, William, *68*
Kimbolton Castle, 9
Kindsay, Sir George, *70*

Labeled Dublin commodes, 8–9
Langlois, Pierre, 13–14
Late Chippendale armchairs, 9
Late Chippendale creations, 8
Late Chippendale examples, 9, 12
Late Chippendale furniture, 9, 12
Late Chippendale mode, 9
Late Chippendale open-fret pattern, 10
Late Chippendale productions, 9
Leeds Art Calendar, 13
Leeds Museum, 13
London, 7, 8, 11–12, 13, 14
London (misnomer), 7, 8
London antique dealers, 8
London antique dealers' advertisements, 8
London designs, 14
London firms, 8
London marquetry, 13
London productions, 14
London publishing industry, 7, 8
Louvre, *37*

Mack, Williams, and Gibton, 8, 9
Macquoid, Percy, 16
Macquoid and Edwards, 16
Martin, Ralph G., 8
Metropolitan Furniture of the Georgian Years,
    12, 13
Moore, James, 15
Moore, William, 16, *123, 130, 139–142, 144*

National Arts Collection Fund, 13
National Museum of Ireland, 9
Needlework, Irish, *12, 49*
New England, 7
New York City, 8, 13
New York origin, 16
New York Public Library, 11
Northern Europe, 7

Oak-leaf-and-acorn carving, *15, 16, 45*
Oak leaves, *62*
Old English Furniture, 7, 8, 17
Ormolu, 12
Ormolu mounts, 12, *133, 142, 167, 171, 172,
    174, 178, 186, 190, 197*

Parisian marquetry, 13
Philadelphia, 15–16, *31*
"Philadelphia," *92, 93*
Popularity, long, of Chippendale
    designs, 12
Populations, records of, 11
Potsdam, 11
Present State of Old English Furniture, 17

Randolph, Benjamin, 16, *31*
Ribband-back armchair, *25, 27*
Ripon, Marquis of, *69*
Royal patronage, 8
Russia, 11

St. Oswald, Lord, 16
Satyr mask, *131*
Scotland, 7, 10
Stockholm, 11
Stratford, Countess of, *49*
Studleigh Royal, *69*
Switzerland, 11
Symonds, R. W., 12, 13, 15, 17, *36*

Tassel splat, Van Renselaer, 16
Tax-free looking glasses, 7

Teahan, John, 9
"To his Majesty," 8
Trevelyan, Lady, 15, *10*
Trewergy Manor, 10

Untermyer, Judge Irwin, 12

Venetian (misnomer), *109*
Victoria & Albert Museum, 12, 13
Vile, William, *68*

Wales, 7, 10
Warwick, Earl of, *152*
Warwick Castle, 15
Warwickshire, *10, 152*
Waterford chandeliers, 11
Welcombe Castle, 15
West Indies, 7
Whorled-together arm terminals
    and arm supports, 15, *6*
Widener, Joseph E., *37*
Williams and Gibton, 9
Wykeham Abbey, *68*

Yew, Irish, *152, 192*
Yorkshire, *68, 69*